RELEASED!

OVERCOMING SEXUAL TRAUMA

WORKBOOK

Paul Helton, Ph.D.

and

Taraleigh Stemler, MMFT

ISBN: 1523426225
ISBN-13: 978-1523426225

Contents

Table of Contents

Acknowledgements

All thanks to the God of all mercies for making so many of my dreams come true. To Dana, my wife, friend and constant source of encouragement thank you for your patience in this and many other endeavors. Special thanks to Holly Rowsey who has been a constant source of help with formatting and design.

Paul G. Helton, Ph.D., LPC, MHSP

To my God for creating me in a wonderful way to connect with hurting people.

To my husband for believing in my abilities despite my self-doubt and encouraging me to always dream big.

To my parents, family, and friends who supported me in my pursuit to enter a field of healing.

To Dr. Paul Helton for the constant support and encouragement as I've grown in becoming a student of humanity's complexities.

Taraleigh Stemler, MMFT

Chapter 1

The Beginning Of The End

Attachment theory finds significance in the parent-child relationship and its influence on the child's physical, emotional, mental, relational, and social development. A child depends solely on the caregiver for regulating his or her needs, such as hunger and thirst or the child's emotional states.

In the first two years of life, a child's brain is undergoing the most brain development it will experience in all the child's life. Neurogenesis and apoptosis take place during this accelerated brain development period. Trauma, abuse, and disruptions to the child's regulatory system may prevent the child's ability to properly regulate emotions, physiological responses, and identity formation.

Psychologist Mary Ainsworth devised an assessment technique called the **Strange Situation Classification** (SSC) in order to investigate how attachments might vary between children. The Strange Situation was devised by Ainsworth & Wittig (1969) and was based on Ainsworth's previous Uganda (1967) and later Baltimore studies (Ainsworth et al., 1971, 1978).

The stories recounted by Katie give the reader a glimpse into her childhood experiences and how her development has progressed. Consider the following questions:

1

1. Make a list of people you trusted as a child? How does trust factor into proper growth

    and development as a human being?

    _____

    _____

    _____

    _____

    _____

    _____

    _____

    _____

    _____

2. What suggestions would you give a person who does not have a friend or relative they

    can trust?

    _____

    _____

    _____

    _____

3. Using on-line searches, list the four types of attachments and provide a brief description

    of each.

    _____

    _____

    _____

    _____

4. What type of attachment style do you believe Katie developed? Please explain.

_____

_____

_____

_____

_____

_____

_____

_____

5. How did this attachment style mold her thinking?

_____

_____

_____

_____

6. How would this style shape her view of Mom and Dad?

_____

_____

_____

_____

7. Using personal reflection and critical thinking skills, what attachment style most accurately describes your attachment style?

_____

_____

_____

_____

8. How do you think this style impacts your view of other people, which may include those from your family, work and even religious group?

_____

_____

_____

_____

9. Define the following terms:

    a. Neurogenesis

_____

_____

    b. Apoptosis

_____

_____

10. How might these different processes affect a person's development and view of

themselves?

_____

_____

_____

_____

11. Katie described herself as a "shell of a person" as a result from the abuse she suffered. How might this belief affect Katie's identity formation?

_____

_____

_____

_____

12. Katie shared she mentally would escape to a "white room" as she was being abused. From a spiritual perspective, explain why you believe going to a "white room" was a significant escape for her. Consider reading I John 1:5-7 in the bible.

_____

_____

_____

_____

13. Patricia DeYoung, the author of *"Understanding and Treating Chronic Shame: A Relational/Neurobiological" Approach*, proposes that shame is the "experience of one's felt sense of self disintegrating in relation to a deregulating other" (DeYoung, 2015, p. 18). After reviewing DeYoung's ideas online, write a brief summary of her ideas related to shame.

_____

_____

_____

_____

_____

_____

_____

_____

14. When recounting her experiences, Katie often uses language that reflects her feelings of unworthiness and unlovable as her experience of self. As a therapist, it is extremely important to recognize this is a deep felt sense of self, not just low self-esteem that needs to change with cognitive skills. If you were working with Katie who felt deep in her core that she was unlovable or unworthy, what action steps might you take as her friend or therapist?

_____

_____

_____

_____

_____

15. When we feel disconnected from our attachment figure (e.g. mother, father, grandmother, etc.) as a child, we experience shame from an egocentric perspective, believing the disconnection has happened because something is inherently wrong with us. As an example, if your spouse was sexually abused as a child, how might you handle arguments or disagreements with your spouse knowing their world was painted by disconnection being "their fault"?

_____

_____

_____

_____

_____

16. Make a list of people you can trust. Who can you trust completely? How does trust in another person enhance a person's life?

_____

_____

_____

_____

17. Other than PTSD what are some secondary symptoms that might accompany a traumatic childhood?

_____

_____

_____

_____

_____

_____

Chapter 2

Loss of Innocence

Eric Erikson's psychosocial developmental stages serve as a useful tool to understand the complexity of one's personal development, and in this case, Katie's development.

1. Locate and list Eric Erikson's eight stages of development with descriptions for each stage:

                    Stage   Description

    a. _____

    b. _____

    c. _____

    d. _____

    e. _____

    f. _____

g. _____

h. _____

2. As you review Erikson's stages, consider your childhood and how particular people may have influenced you in a positive or negative way. Who was the most positive influence in your childhood? List the reasons.

_____

_____

_____

_____

3. Who most negatively impacted your childhood? You may find you need to list more than one person. List the reasons.

_____

_____

_____

_____

4. Consider Katie's first memory of being 4 years old and remembering her father sexually

    abusing her on a bed. As a 4 year old, according to Erikson's model, Katie faced the

    developmental milestone of autonomy versus shame and doubt. It is amazing to read

    about Katie recalling a childhood experience before anyone taught her right from wrong.

    Very early in life she had an inclination to feel ashamed as her father sexually abused her.

    Conscience begins at a very early age. Please do an online search on conscience and

    evaluate its role in identity formation.

    _____

    _____

    _____

    _____

5. From an attachment perspective, the caregiver is to provide safety and comfort for the child. Unfortunately, Katie's father exploited her during a very early stage and a vulnerable age. Therefore, the natural reaction Katie felt was shame. She doubted that she is worthy of love. These ideas began to dominate her view of self. What symptoms might a child display at school that could be mistaken by teachers as a "bad attitude?"

_____

_____

_____

_____

6. Another memory Katie recalled at age 10 when her cousins and brother forced her to perform oral sex on them occurred during the developmental stage of industry versus inferiority. Look up this particular stage and summarize the impact of how being forced into premature sexuality impedes the normal functioning of a child.

_____

_____

_____

_____

7. Forcing Katie into an inferior position created feelings of powerlessness over her circumstances. According to Erikson, children need to form intimate, loving relationships with other people. Success leads to strong relationships, while failure results in loneliness and isolation. The result leads to a skewed view of one's importance and value of themselves and others. For more details, consider exploring the following website for more information on Erikson ideas related to stages of development.

http://psychology.about.com/od/psychosocialtheories/fl/Psychosocial-Stages-Summary-Chart.htm.

_____

_____

_____

_____

_____

_____

_____

8. How does sexual trauma impact sexual intimacy?

_____

_____

_____

_____

_____

_____

_____

_____

9. The narrative created for Katie associated pain, fear, shame, and loneliness with sexual intimacy or feeling like a sexual being. As a therapist or friend, how might you work with her to create a new framework for how she views sexuality and sexual intimacy with her spouse?

_____

_____

_____

_____

10. According to Bessel van der Kolk's "*The Body Keeps the Score*", physical touch is a key variable impacted by a history of abuse. What can be problematic areas later in Katie's life?

_____

_____

_____

_____

In Louis Cozolino's book, "*The Neuroscience of Human Relationships*", ways of attaching to others can be summed up in the statement, "The first thing we learn about our caretakers is how well they are able to make us feel calm and safe" (Cozolino, 2014, p. 143). Katie identified her "normal" as being "abnormal". Describe in your own words the ways Katie's "abnormal" can have negative long-term consequences intra-personally and inter-personally.

11. Clients who have a history of sexual abuse and trauma oftentimes struggle facing the facts of their abuse. Reliving the details of the abuse can be a daunting task while working with a therapist. Bessel van der Kolk stated, "What is critical is that the patients themselves learn to tolerate feeling what they feel and knowing what they know" (van der Kolk, 2014, p. 125). Discuss the rationale behind why this would be a crucial step for the client in therapy?

_____

_____

_____

_____

"The Body Keeps The Score", written by Bessel van der Kolk, is an educational resource on developmental trauma, its effects on the brain, and its impact on relationships.

12. Watch the following video and write your thoughts on how you understand developmental

trauma on the brain and relationships: https://www.youtube.com/watch?v=53RX2ESIqsM

_____

_____

_____

_____

13. Language is developed in the parietal lobe of the brain and can reflect an individual's

intra-psychic processes. "The Sexual Healing Journey" uses the term "survivor" to

describe an individual who suffered from sexual abuse and trauma. Considering how

language can reflect intra-psychic processes. Why might the author choose to use the

term "survivor" compared to "victim"?

_____

_____

_____

_____

According to Patricia DeYoung, "attachment trauma is also a right-brain, emotional phenomenon" (DeYoung, 2015, p. 37), impacting parts of the brain responsible for emotion expressed relationally through eye contact, voice tone, and subtle body movements.

14. If you are a therapist working with a client who has experienced attachment trauma, including sexual abuse, what might you do with this client to help him/her?

_____

_____

_____

_____

_____

A valuable resource that many individuals and couples affected by sexual abuse have utilized is, *"The Sexual Healing Journey: A Guide for Survivors of Sexual Abuse"* by Wendy Maltz. Providing a Sexual Effects Inventory, the book includes chapters on automatic reactions due to the abuse, acknowledging the abuse, creating a new meaning for sex, and finding healing with an intimate partner.

15. How does a person make a positive change in their personality especially when shame, guilt and the feelings of being unloved were engrained early?

_____

_____

_____

_____

_____

Chapter 3

Becoming Fatherless

Validating one's emotional experiences (EFT) is an important piece of how emotional security and safety is built between people. If a parent tells a child "Don't be scared" when the child is scared, that is invalidating to the child, feeling as if something is wrong with them with the experience of being afraid. This can destroy a child's autonomy and identity, feeling ashamed even for what they think or feel.

1. Reflect and review Eric Erikson's psychosocial developmental stages and determine whether or not a child who is experiencing an identity crisis can be redirected. If so, what course of action would a caregiver need to take to ensure success for a child in crisis?

_____

_____

_____

_____

Katie shared that her first memory of abuse was when she was 4 years old. Using Erikson's psychosocial developmental stages chart, explain how problems might be exhibited in Katie's behaviors, cognitions, or relationships.

2. Draw Maslow's hierarchy of needs including 5 levels. Include 3 areas that fit each level. For example, on the physiological level, it would include food, water, clothing and shelter.

_____

_____

_____

_____

_____

3.   It is important to note that in, Maslow's hierarchy; unless the basic needs of the bottom of the inverted triangle are met then the individual does not move progress and move forward. Each and every stage is important as it leads to self-actualization. At what point did Katie stall in her growth according to this model?

_____

_____

_____

_____

In the book, Katie mentions aligning her beliefs with Christianity throughout her lifetime. In Christianity, the Bible remains the main source of wisdom, guidance, and comfort for all life's situations. One particular verse in the New Testament, Matthew 11:28-30, speaks about the "soul". Interestingly, the Greek translation of "soul" in that verse is "psyche", which is another word used for "the mind".

4. If Jesus Christ protects one's soul, can that mean He protects one's emotional and mental wellbeing as well as their mind? Write one paragraph of your personal thoughts.

_____

_____

_____

_____

5. Katie uses the metaphor of being like a soldier in a war zone during the sexual abuse at the hands of family members. If you were a therapist working with Katie, why might using metaphors help the therapeutic process?

_____

_____

_____

_____

From early childhood, Katie's relationship with her father was tainted with everything but intimacy, care, and love for her wellbeing. According to neuroscience research, Cozolino quotes Taylor & Repetti (pg. 238), "Unhealthy environments, such as those that are chronically stressful, conflictual, and abusive, create unhealthy brains and bodies". Sadly, Katie represents a great majority of children who grow up in abusive homes and carry the mental baggage for all their lives.

"The Neuroscience of Human Relationships" speaks about some mental health professionals (Cohen, 2004; Rook, 1984; Seeman, 1996) speculating that, "negative relationships can have more destructive effects on the body than positive relationships have to be healing".

6.   How might the previous statement be valid?

_____

_____

_____

_____

_____

Recognize the importance of a father in a child's life. Particularly for Katie, her father was the first experience she would have with a man on this earth. Unfortunately, that first experience with a man - her father - was sexual, beyond anything she could comprehend, and because of these early sexual experiences with her father, she immediately felt shame as her identity.

7. Isn't it interesting that sexual abuse causes children to feel that something isn't right? If yes, please explain.

_____

_____

_____

_____

_____

Matthew 18:1-6 emphasizes Jesus' perspective on being like children. For adults who neglect or abuse their children, who do not provide ultimate care and connection for children, they set the children up to "sin" or experience lack of security, safety, and healthy connection in the world, tainting their picture of how life can be. Intimate connection, being known, seen, heard, and understood is the fantasy, not the reality to be lived out or experienced fully.

8. Dr. Edward Tronick, a developmental psychologist, developed the Still Face Experiment. It demonstrates the phenomenon of responsive versus non-responsive mother-child interactions and its impact on a child's social cognition and engagement. Watch the "Still Face Experiment: Dr. Edward Tronick" 2:49 minute video. After watching the video, how might this play a role given the sexual abuse Katie endured during her child development?

_____

_____

_____

_____

_____

9. How do your present relationships positively or negatively impact your life?

_____

_____

_____

_____

_____

_____

_____

_____

Chapter 4

No Way, No Hope

Bessel van der Kolk writes, "One of the ways the memory of helplessness is stored is as muscle tension or feelings of disintegration in the affected body areas: head, back, and limbs in accident victims, vagina and rectum in victims of sexual abuse" (2014, p. 265).

1. In addition, Louis Cozolino states, "There may also be a tendency to convert emotional stress into physical symptoms" (2014, p. 389). Using on on-line search of the available charts and the above statements, explain why it would be a likely chance that Katie experienced an anxiety attack at an early age.

_____

_____

_____

_____

Narrative therapy is a type of treatment therapist's use with clients that allows clients to write out their stories, revisit disturbing memories, and narrate their future. Louis Cozolino (2014, p. 392) writes on this subject by saying, "Our own personal narratives contribute to our reactions, responses, and ways of engaging with others".

2. Have you ever told someone the truth only to be told that you were lying? How did that make you feel?

_____

_____

_____

_____

3. If you were a therapist working with Katie and using narrative therapy, what themes might be found in Katie's narrative?

_____

_____

_____

Katie mentions she makes her first friend around age 11. Sadly, the friendship is cut short when the friend moves away. Using the appropriate charts, explain why this unfortunate event would greatly devastate her as an 11-year-old girl.

Katie expressed growing up she desperately wanted someone to find out what was happening to her but felt pressure to keep the abuse a secret. In Chapter 4, she talks about finally telling her mother about how she was being hurt by her brother. Her mother's response was, "You probably deserved it!" Louis Cozolino (2014, p. 399) shares, "And when the drive to love is thwarted - when we are frightened, abused, or neglected - our mental health is compromised".

4. What beliefs might Kate have developed about herself, others, and how the world works according to the above information?

_____

_____

_____

_____

Bessel van der Kolk (2014, p. 233) in Chapter 14 talks about language and breaking the silence that isolates trauma survivors. "Hiding core feelings takes an enormous amount of energy, it saps your motivation to pursue worthwhile goals, and it leaves you feeling bored and shut down. Meanwhile, stress hormones keep flooding your body, leading to headaches, muscle aches, problems with your bowels or sexual functions". "Ignoring inner reality also eats away at your sense of self, identity, and purpose". "Only the system devoted to self-awareness, which is based in the medial prefrontal cortex, can change the emotional brain".

In Katie's accounts, it appears that her relationships with her mother and father do not provide her with safety, security, and comfort. According to Cozolino's, *"The Neuroscience of Healthy Relationships"* (2014, p. 277), he claims interpersonal trauma places children in a difficult position - "they want to cling to another for support while pushing him or her away for protection".

Psychologist Mary Ainsworth was a key individual in further identifying different attachment styles using the assessment technique called the Strange Situation Classification. This assessment was used to examine how attachments might differ between children. Watch "The Strange Situation - Mary Ainsworth" 3:14 minute video.

5. Shame researcher Brene Brown has written many pieces of shame, its nature, and how it leaves us isolated from connection. As a resource, watch Brene Brown's youtube video, "Brene Brown: Listening to Shame" 20:39 minute video. As you watch the video record the notes and look for common themes within Katie's story.

_____

_____

_____

_____

_____

Chapter 5

Escape to Fantasyland

1. Katie's experience of leaving home and going to college can be considered part of the "emerging into adulthood" life cycle stage. Look up the family life cycle and list all the stages with a brief 1-2 sentence description of what occurs in each stage.

_____

_____

_____

_____

2. Look back to Erikson's psychosocial developmental stages. Which stage does Katie fall under during this time in her life?

_____

_____

_____

_____

_____

3. What obstacles does she face considering her abuse history in conjunction with the psychosocial crisis she faces?

_____

_____

_____

_____

_____

Katie mentions that she finally could sleep peacefully without feeling the urge to stay awake for fear of being abused at night. According to Bessel van der Kolk's work, traumatized individuals are more apt to suffering from sleep disorders due to the constant hyper-arousal of mind and body.

4.   What part of the brain is responsible for the fight-flight-freeze response?

_____

_____

_____

_____

5.   Describe the physiological mechanisms of action as to how the fight-flight-freeze is triggered?

_____

_____

_____

_____

6. How could this part of the brain negatively impact a healthy sleep pattern?

_____

_____

_____

_____

7. What are some ways you can calm racing thoughts in order to sleep?

_____

_____

_____

_____

8. Map out the central nervous system (CNS) and autonomic nervous system (ANS) in the brain. Include a brief 1-2 sentence description for what is considered part of each system and the function of each part in the system. In the ANS, include the sympathetic and parasympathetic systems.

    _____

    _____

    _____

    _____

    _____

9. The process of being honest and open with one another, especially in a dating or marital relationship, is key to creating emotional safety and security and, therefore, reinforces the ability to be seen, heard, and understood by one another. What might a person, like Katie, with a history of abuse need to look for in another person to feel emotionally safe before sharing their history?

    _____

    _____

    _____

    _____

In Marnie Ferree's "No Stones: Women Redeemed From Sexual Addiction", she addresses the core beliefs a female sex addict, or any addict, adopts due to experiences of trauma or abandonment as a child.

1   I am a bad, unworthy person.
2   No one would love me as I am.
3   No one will meet my needs.
4   Sex or a relationship is my most important need.

Notice the restricting nature of the abovementioned statements. The ultimate conclusion for such events to occur is because of a "bad" nature. No one would love the person as they are or ever meet the person's needs.

Sex or a relationship carries all the weight of that person surviving day to day because it is the ultimate need to fulfill.

The first experience of disconnection occurred in the Garden of Eden between God, man & woman. God had seen his creation, especially creating connection between man and woman as very good. He wouldn't have wasted his time creating such beings if He didn't love them fully. He placed them in the ultimate haven where all their needs were met (food, drink, shelter, purpose, relationship).

Their ultimate need of connection with God and with one another existed in an optimal way. However, as I Corinthians 1 states, the people traded the truth of God for a lie. When Adam & Eve gave into temptation and traded the truth they knew and experienced with God for a lie from the serpent, they immediately experienced disconnection, ultimately shame of who they were.

Though they may have not qualified as addicts, the ultimate disconnection from God resulted in the four core beliefs addicts experience - they were ashamed of who they were so they covered themselves, their eyes were opened, they knew they were naked, they hid themselves from God, and all of a sudden, the beautiful communion with God that Adam & Eve experienced turned into Adam's response "I was afraid (when he heard the sound of God) and hid myself".

Blaming officially enters the scene of humanity as Adam passively participated in the sin. He quickly blames God by labeling Eve as "the woman you gave to me". Adam's original response about Eve was "This AT LAST is bone of my bones, and flesh of my flesh". Marriage was immediately ripped apart. The response after sin was to immediately place blame (responsibility) elsewhere.

Interestingly, God states in Genesis 3:22, "Behold, the man has become like one of us in knowing good and evil". It seems to be that God's intention was ultimately what we experience as a child - innocence. That God wished to provide ultimate care for His "children" in their "home" that was "safe and secure" and that cultivated "connection". Luke 18:15-17 portrays Jesus' thoughts on children and how significant they are. If we don't receive the kingdom of God like a child, what must that mean if we receive the kingdom of God with an adult mind, filled with toxins of self-doubt, shame, guilt, hatred, and inconsistent thoughts about God's nature.

10. When we think about shame, we have to consider the isolation that naturally comes with it, causing us to disconnect from social relationships. Reflecting on your personal experience with your "self", what are ways you may "escape to fantasyland" or "numb yourself" due to shame you feel?

_____

_____

_____

_____

_____

_____

Chapter 6

Dying to Live

Coping skills are an area that a therapist will oftentimes assist a client in developing and strengthening for stable emotional and mental health.

From an attachment theory perspective, our caregiver teaches a child how to self-soothe by soothing the child when the child is crying or is hungry. There are a variety of coping skills that humans will adopt, such as avoidance, crying spells, and binge-eating.

1. Unfortunately for Katie, one of her coping skills was self-harm by cutting. Look up "The Cornell Research Program on Self-Injury and Recovery", find "Resources for" headline, click on the "Friends" tab, and read the following: "How can I help a friend who self-injures?"

_____

_____

_____

_____

2. 15 Misconceptions

a. _____

b. _____

c. _____

d. _____

e. _____

f. _____

g. _____

h. _____

i. _____

j. _____

k. _____

l. _____

m. _____

n. _____

o. _____

3. How can self injuring behaviors become addictive? Please explain your answer.

_____

_____

_____

_____

_____

_____

_____

4. Self-injury in the media

_____

_____

_____

_____

_____

5. Respectful curiosity

_____

_____

_____

_____

_____

Internal Family Systems Therapy, known as IFS, is a particular therapeutic approach to treating clients, such as Cognitive-Behavioral Therapy or Structural Therapy. In "The Body Keeps the Score", van der Kolk states, the "core of IRS is the notion that the mind of each of us is like a family in which the members have different levels of maturity, excitability, wisdom, and pain. The parts form a network or system in which change in any one part will affect all the others" (2014, p. 281).

6. Go to www.selfleadership.org, find the "About Internal Family System" section, and read the following:
   - Managers, Firefighters, and Exiles
   - The Self
   - The Self-Led Person
   - Qualities of the Self

   a. How do managers, firefighters and exiles assist us in coping with traumatic events?

   _____

   _____

   _____

   _____

   _____

b. How is the self defined?

_____

_____

_____

_____

c. How does a better understanding of one's self help one in therapy related to trauma?

_____

_____

_____

_____

d. Using Internal Family Systems

_____

_____

_____

_____

_____

e. In your own words describe a self-led person?

_____

_____

_____

_____

f. In a crisis or stressful situation, how would a self-led person respond?

_____

_____

_____

_____

g. What qualities do you possess that are self-led?

_____

_____

_____

_____

_____

h. List the eight C's of Self-Leadership.

1) _____

2) _____

3) _____

4) _____

5) _____

6) _____

7) _____

8) _____

Chapter 7

Wrestling with the Almighty

Many people use spirituality as a resource for improving themselves or to sense a greater purpose in life. Unfortunately, some survivors of abuse will struggle with spirituality, seeing it more as an area confusion rather than comfort. Particularly for Katie, her Christian beliefs were tainted and flawed, causing her to question God, His nature, and the extent to which He cared for her.

1. If you were a therapist working with Katie on this particular spiritual issue - that is her view of God being a loving Father to her - how would you allow Katie to explore this area without unethically forcing her to believe God loves her or cares for her?

---

2. Katie stated in this chapter, "My mind limits God with what I feel is true but not the truth".

   In your own words, explain what you think Katie is saying in this comment.

   _____

   _____

   _____

   _____

   _____

3. In what way is it important to allow clients to sit in their grief or pain and ask "why"

   questions regarding their abuse or suffering?

   _____

   _____

   _____

   _____

Consider Maslow's hierarchy of needs, particularly the level of self-actualization. From previous resources provided in this workbook and building on previous statements about shame, we understand the isolating nature of shame, preventing us from healthy, authentic connection.

4. How might one's relationship with their Higher Power be impacted by chronic shame brought on by a history of sexual abuse?

5. What recommendations for solace could you give to a person who does not believe in God or isn't ready to trust God?

_____

_____

_____

_____

_____

Chapter 8

Trying, Tiring, and Turbulent Therapy

In *"The Neuroscience of Human Relationships"*, Cozolino remarks, "The dynamics of some families may even make it dangerous to experience one's own feelings. Attending to and articulating feelings are learned abilities that require the involvement, support, and encouragement of those around us" (2014, p. 73).

The back-to-back accounts Katie describes of opening up to a therapist about her abuse and the therapist not providing emotional safety or ethical services is a poor reflection on the mental health community. In some respect, the way each therapist treated her only solidified in Katie's mind the brutal reality that she is the problem or is a waste of the therapist's time.

1. For personal reflection, write a paragraph describing what it would feel like to be, in Katie's words, "less than human".

_____

_____

_____

_____

As Dr. Paul Helton highlights throughout this chapter, it is crucial for a therapist to understand his or her limitations and know when it is an appropriate time to refer to another professional that can help the client more efficiently.

2. From a clinical perspective, state some specific reasons that therapists should treat the referral process with clients gently when referring them to another therapist?

_____

_____

_____

_____

3. How would you encourage someone who has been abused to seek help without being too demanding?

_____

_____

_____

_____

Chapter 9

Out of the Shadows

Dr. Paul Helton briefly talks about perception regarding Katie's comment, "So you don't hate me?" after reading her journal. In "The Body Keeps the Score", van der Kolk dedicates a whole chapter to discussing how neurofeedback is used to rewire the brain, particularly for soldiers and trauma patients. His remark is valid regarding changing the brain when he wrote, "The challenge in PTSD is to open the mind to new possibilities, so that the present is no longer interpreted as a continuous reliving of the past" (2014, p. 326).

1. As Dr. Paul Helton commented, could Katie just simply believe the reality that she is worthy and lovable into existence or is perception a deeply-ingrained cognitive process that is a result from the brain's physiology? Write your reaction to this question. As Katie mentioned, she felt as if her previous therapist had merely shipped her off to a psychiatric treatment center to be rid of her and placed on medication. Medication is an incredible resource that has saved millions of lives and, in particular, has slowly started to make an impact in the mental health field. However, van der Kolk's research found that "between 75 percent and 80 percent of patients who are admitted for detox and alcohol and drug abuse treatment will relapse" (2014, p. 327). Through his practice and multiple studies, he has observed there is a cyclical pattern between PTSD and substance abuse. He notes, "There are only two ways to end this vicious cycle: by resolving the symptoms of PTSD

with methods such as EMDR or by treating the hyper-arousal that is part of both PTSD

and withdrawal from drugs or alcohol" (van der Kolk, 2014, p. 327).

_____

_____

_____

_____

_____

2. Visit emdr.com and provide the name and description of EMDR. Then state the rationale

behind the Adaptive Information Processing Model.

_____

_____

_____

_____

Louis Cozolino writes about experience-dependent plasticity, which "denotes that our brains are structured and restructured by interactions with our social and natural environments".

Research quoted in Cozolino's, *"The Neuroscience of Human Relationships"* supports that "early interactions build neural networks and establish biological set points that can last a lifetime". Therefore, parenting is elevated to a higher standard because inevitably the caretakers "activate the growth of the brain through emotional availability and reciprocal interactions" (Cozolino, 2014, p. 82).

3. Knowing how intricately connected the relationships and a body's physiological processes are, what do you believe would help Katie the most - medication, relationships, or combination of both? Please give a detailed response for your answer.

_____

_____

_____

_____

_____

_____

_____

Chapter 10

Long and Winding Road

Dr. Paul Helton comments on his observations of Katie's behavior when he asked her about forgiving others for wrongdoing. Katie's verbal and nonverbal cues communicated that the trauma was so devastating that words would not do it justice. Her affect and body language showed the trauma was trapped within her body at a very deep level.

1. Van der Kolk's book discusses how traumatized individuals often have "poorly modulated autonomic nervous systems" because they "are easily thrown off balance, both mentally and physically" by non-threatening stimuli, such as a simple question of "How have you been wronged?"

_____

_____

_____

_____

Visit yoga activist.org and read "Yoga for Trauma Survivors".

2. How does yoga help a trauma survivor physically and mentally?

_____

_____

_____

_____

3. How do they incorporate language into the yoga class?

_____

_____

_____

_____

4. List 5 physical expressions of possible dissociation and emotional triggers in children.

1) _____

2) _____

3) _____

4) _____

5) _____

5. Briefly explain in 1-2 paragraphs your perspective on yoga benefits for trauma after reading the article.

_____

_____

_____

_____

From an attachment perspective combined with spirituality, one could theorize that Katie's attachment style to her caregivers, particularly her parents, may reflect her attachment style to God.

6. Looking back at the attachment style chart, how would you describe her attachment to God?

_____

_____

_____

_____

_____

7. From a spiritual standpoint, why might this information be important to know if you're a therapist working with a Christian who claims his or her faith is a resource for them but may not be seeing improvement?

_____

_____

_____

_____

8. Look up and read "Attachment by Jesus" by Alice Stricklin. This is spiritual resource for clients who are receiving EMDR treatments and identify spirituality as an important part of their healing process. List and describe the key elements within the article by Stricklin.

_____

_____

_____

_____

_____

Chapter 11

Making Sense Out of Non-Sense

One reason that Katie experienced success in therapy with Dr. Paul Helton was largely due to the therapeutic relationship. According to research on outcomes in therapy, the therapeutic relationship between therapist and client represents 30 percent of the success clients experience in therapy. Louis Cozolino notes, "The major implication for psychotherapy from all these findings is that insecure attachment is subject to change as a result of positive social input" (Cozolino, 2014, p. 334).

1. Considering the previous statement, what aspects of the therapeutic relationship do you believe accounted for Katie's therapy success compared to her previous therapists?

_____

_____

_____

_____

Harry Harlow was a psychologist who theorized about human behavior and development through experiments using monkeys. One particular experiment of significant proportion was Harlow's experiment using infant monkeys and surrogate mothers. Harlow created two different surrogate mothers - one was made of heavy wire mesh and the other made of wood covered with cloth. The infant monkeys "raised" by the wire surrogate mothers gradually presented with self-abusive and autistic behaviors, such as rocking back and forth or clutching to themselves. Though the wire surrogate mothers were the source of food and warmth provided by an electric light, these infant monkeys would spend a greater amount of time clinging to the cloth surrogate mother.

2.   Watch "Harry Harlow Monkey Experiment Contact Comfort" 2:06 minute video. Record your notes below.

_____

_____

_____

_____

_____

In creating one's narrative, Cozolino wrote "Most of us also find it helpful to develop a narrative of our own lives to help us reflect upon our past experiences and guide us toward the future. This ability to think of ourselves in the third person is essentially constructing a

TOM (theory of mind) by viewing our own experience from an objective perspective" (2014, p. 372).

Katie expressed how difficult it was to feel her own feelings or think for herself, not wanting to upset anyone around her. Trauma oftentimes causes a person to be "stuck" at the cognitive and emotional age of the abuse.

For Katie, this would be 4 years old and at a time when she couldn't fully verbalize her feelings of the abuse nor describe the extent to which she was violated.

Using writing in therapy sessions for Katie to express her thoughts only speaks volumes to the quoted statement in Cozolino's book, "There is evidence that narratives foster emotional security while minimizing the need for elaborate psychological defenses" (2014, p. 389).

3. Accessing your personal reflections, why might it be easier to write their feelings rather than to speak them?

_____

_____

_____

_____

4. Read "The Covenant Community Web" by Alice Stricklin. This is a resource created for clients as the therapist and client prepare to do EMDR sessions for trauma cases. Briefly outline the main points giving a short description for each point.

_____

_____

_____

_____

_____

Chapter 12

Effective Treatment Begins

Core shame can be seen as an underlying theme for Katie's history of sexual abuse.

Developing her sense of self and making decisions for her life was an overwhelming task.

She also bore the fear that she would upset others. Her identity formation was so closely

attached to her childhood experiences, her interactions with her parents, family members,

and the social norms of her family and community systems.

Cozolino speaks to core shame, stating it's not related to behaviors but more "to the

experience of the self". Furthermore, Cozolino believes "core shame is the visceral experience

of being disconnected, shunned, and expelled from social connectedness, stimulating the

same brain regions activated during pain" (2014, p. 283).

1. From a Christian perspective, how might core shame be problematic for one's faith and

    relationship with God?

_____

_____

_____

_____

_____

Shame is described in the Bible as a state of being ONLY with the wicked (Proverbs 13:5).

Everywhere else in the Bible shame is considered a state of being that Christians do not have

to experience because of the beauty of the gospel.

Ashamed is an adjective of how one feels about the actions they took. Shame has never been

something that God caused His children to experience of who they were, but rather more

feeling ashamed by their actions (turning to other gods, not believing in His power, etc).

Cozolino's research found that children develop self-awareness between ages 5-10 years old,

meaning "positive self-esteem or core shame have already been programmed as social and

emotional givens" (2014, p. 285).

Consider Maslow's hierarchy of needs and Erikson's psychosocial developmental stages.

Also think about one's spiritual development throughout life.

2. Provide a personal reflection on your experience with positive self-esteem or core shame and how this has impacted your identity formation, spiritual development, and social relationships.

_____

_____

_____

_____

_____

3. What message(s) would you would like to instill in your children that were not communicated to you during your childhood?

_____

_____

_____

_____

_____

4. Read "Nine Things Educators Need to Know About the Brain" by Louis Cozolino. List each point with a brief description. How might this transform one's perspective on parenting or teaching children?

_____

_____

_____

_____

_____

References

Cozolino, L. (2014). (2nd ed.). *The neuroscience of healthy relationships: Attachment and the developing social brain*. W. W. Norton & Company: New York, NY.

DeYoung, P. (2015). *Understanding and treating chronic shame: A relational/neurobiological approach*. Routledge: New York, NY.

Ferree, M. C. (2010). *No stones: Women redeemed from sexual addiction*. InterVarsity Press: Madison, WI.

Maltz, W. (2012). (3rd ed.). *The sexual healing journey: A guide for survivors of sexual abuse*. HarperCollins Publishers: New York, NY.

"Scripture quotations are from the ESV® Bible (The Holy Bible, English Standard Version®), copyright © 2001 by Crossway, a publishing ministry of Good News Publishers. Used by permission. All rights reserved."

Van der Kolk, B. (2014). *The body keeps the score: Brain, mind, and body in the healing of trauma*. Penguin Group: New York, NY

www.ingramcontent.com/pod-product-compliance
Lightning Source LLC
Chambersburg PA
CBHW081410280526
45788CB00009B/3042